BIOFUEL ENERGY

PUTTING PLANTS TO WORK

JESSIE ALKIRE

Consulting Editor, Diane Craig, M.A./Reading Specialist

Super Sandcastle

An Imprint of Abdo Publishing
abdopublishing.com

abdopublishing.com

Printed in the United States of America, North Mankato, Minnesota

052018
092018

THIS BOOK CONTAINS
RECYCLED MATERIALS

Design and Production: Mighty Media, Inc.
Editor: Megan Borgert-Spaniol
Cover Photographs: iStockphoto; Shutterstock; Wikimedia Commons
Interior Photographs: Alamy; iStockphoto; Mariordo/Wikimedia Commons; Mighty Media, Inc.; Shutterstock; Wikimedia Commons

Library of Congress Control Number: 2017961829

Publisher's Cataloging-in-Publication Data
Names: Alkire, Jessie, author.
Title: Biofuel energy: Putting plants to work / by Jessie Alkire.
Other titles: Putting plants to work
Description: Minneapolis, Minnesota : Abdo Publishing, 2019. | Series: Earth's
    energy innovations
Identifiers: ISBN 9781532115691 (lib.bdg.) | ISBN 9781532156410 (ebook)
Subjects: LCSH: Biomass energy--Juvenile literature. | Power resources--
    Juvenile literature. | Energy development--Juvenile literature. | Energy
    conversion--Juvenile literature.
Classification: DDC 333.9539--dc23

Super SandCastle™ books are created by a team of professional educators, reading specialists, and content developers around five essential components—phonemic awareness, phonics, vocabulary, text comprehension, and fluency—to assist young readers as they develop reading skills and strategies and increase their general knowledge. All books are written, reviewed, and leveled for guided reading, early reading intervention, and Accelerated Reader™ programs for use in shared, guided, and independent reading and writing activities to support a balanced approach to literacy instruction.

CONTENTS

WHAT IS BIOFUEL ENERGY?

Biofuel is fuel made from living things. It is often made from plants. It has energy. Burning biofuel **releases** the energy.

Biofuel is renewable. This is because new plants grow quickly. But growing them uses energy and land. This can harm the **environment**.

Plants that are turned into fuel are called biomass. Corn is commonly used as biomass.

ENERGY TIMELINE

1700s–1800s

Vegetable oil is burned
for lighting.

1892

Rudolf Diesel patents
the diesel engine.
It runs on biofuel.

1908

Henry Ford starts
selling the Model T.
It can run on biofuel.

Discover how biofuel energy has changed over time!

1970s-1980s

Petroleum costs rise.
Scientists study biofuels.

2000s

Biofuel is added to
US **gasoline**.

2016

Biofuel produces
5 percent of US energy.

THE FIRST FUEL

The first biofuel used by humans was wood. It was burned for heat. Vegetable oil was another early biofuel. It was burned for lighting in the 1700s and 1800s.

Rudolf Diesel invented the diesel engine in 1892. It ran on biofuel. Henry Ford's Model T car came out in 1908. It could also run on biofuel.

Ford Model T

RUDOLF DIESEL

BORN: March 18, 1858, Paris, France

DIED: September 29, 1913, at sea in the English Channel

Rudolf Diesel was a German engineer. He invented the diesel engine. He patented it in 1892. The engine could be fueled by peanut or vegetable oil. Later models ran on **petroleum**. There were more than 70,000 diesel engines by 1912. They are still used in trucks and trains today!

CLEANER FUEL

Fossil fuels were cheaper than biofuels in the early 1900s. This changed in the 1970s. **Petroleum** costs went up. Also, people started worrying about pollution from burning fossil fuels.

Scientists explored biofuels in the 1980s. Biofuel was added to US **gasoline** in the 2000s. This helped **vehicles** produce less pollution.

Gasoline is a petroleum product.

Most US gasoline today includes about 10 percent biofuel.

SLOW GROWTH

Tractors powered by fossil fuels cause pollution.

Biofuel is still studied today. But **fossil fuels** are used more. Biofuel produced only 5 percent of US energy in 2016.

Growing plants for biofuel can harm the **environment**. Farming machines produce pollution. Clearing land for biofuel plants destroys **habitats**. It also competes with food production. Using land to grow biofuel plants means there is less open land to grow food plants.

Forest habitats are destroyed to grow oil palms. These plants are used for biofuel.

ETHANOL AND BIODIESEL

One common biofuel is ethanol. It is made from plants that have sugar or **starch**. Another biofuel is biodiesel. It is made from plant oils or animal fats. These biofuels power **vehicles**.

Biofuels are also burned for heat. People still burn wood for direct heat. Power plants also burn biofuels. This provides energy to make electricity.

Bus powered by electric and biodiesel fuel engines

In Europe, biodiesel is commonly made from the oils of a yellow plant called rapeseed.

BIOFUEL PRODUCTION

Most biofuels are produced from plants. These plants include corn and sugarcane. They are grown for their **starches** and sugars. Soybeans and oil palms are also common biofuel crops. They are used for their oil.

Sugarcane and corn are **fermented** to make ethanol. Plant oils are processed to make biodiesel.

Sugarcane

Most US ethanol is made from corn.

BURNING FOR POWER

Biofuels are often added to other fuels. Ethanol is added to **gasoline**. Then it is burned to power **vehicles**. Some vehicles can run on ethanol alone!

Power plants burn wood, grass, and other biofuels. The heat produced changes water into steam. The steam turns a **turbine**, which powers a generator. This is a machine that creates electricity.

Car powered by gasoline and ethanol

BIOFUEL POWER PLANT

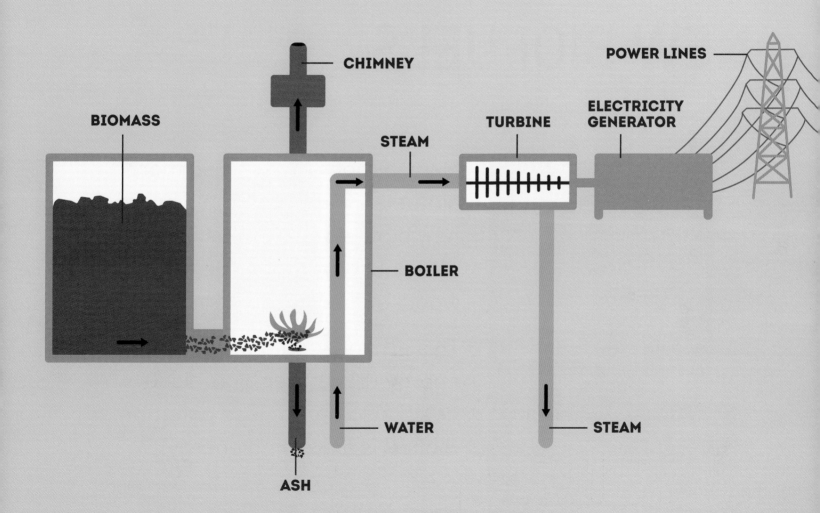

NEW BIOFUELS

Many nations plan to use more biofuels. Scientists also explore new biofuels. One is cellulosic ethanol. It can be made from wood, grasses, and plant waste.

This ethanol could produce more energy than other biofuels. It could also create less pollution. Biofuel is a growing energy!

Cellulosic ethanol can be made from wood chips.

Producing cellulosic ethanol does not compete with food production. It can be made from unused parts of plants grown for food.

MORE ABOUT BIOFUEL ENERGY

Do you want to tell others about biofuel energy? Here are some fun facts to share!

BIODIESEL CAN BE MADE from used cooking oil.

BRAZIL AND THE UNITED STATES produce most of the world's ethanol.

MOST CARS SOLD IN BRAZIL can run on 100 percent ethanol.

TEST YOUR KNOWLEDGE

1. What was the first biofuel?

2. When did Rudolf Diesel invent the diesel engine?

3. Ethanol can be made from corn. **TRUE OR FALSE?**

THINK ABOUT IT!

Look at the plants in your town or city. Can they be made into biofuel?

ANSWERS: 1. Wood 2. 1892 3. True

GLOSSARY

environment – nature and everything in it, such as the land, sea, and air.

ferment – to undergo a chemical process that turns sugar into other products.

fossil fuel – a fuel formed from the remains of plants or animals. Coal, oil, and natural gas are fossil fuels.

gasoline – a liquid that can burn that is used to power engines.

habitat – the area or environment where a person or animal usually lives.

petroleum – a dark-colored liquid that is a fossil fuel. It is used to make gasoline and other fuels.

release – to set free or let go.

starch – a white matter that is found in plants such as potatoes, corn, and rice.

turbine – a machine that produces power when it is rotated at high speed.

vehicle – something used to carry persons or large objects. Examples include cars, trucks, and buses.